the driving people

Pass the MoT test!

How to check & prepare your
car for the annual MoT test

T0124823

Also from Veloce Publishing –

Caring for your bicycle – How to maintain & repair your bicycle (Henshaw)
Caring for your car – How to maintain & service your car (Fry)
Caring for your scooter – How to maintain & service your 49cc to 125cc twist & go
    scooter (Fry)
Dogs on wheels – Travelling with your canine companion (Mort)
Electric Cars – The Future is Now! (Linde)
First aid for your car – Your expert guide to common problems & how to fix them (Collins)
How your car works – Your guide to the components & systems of modern cars,
    including hybrid & electric vehicles (Linde)
How your motorcycle works – Your guide to the components & systems of modern motorcycles
    (Henshaw)
Land Rover Series I-III – Your expert guide to common problems & how to fix them
    (Thurman)
Motorcycles – A first-time-buyer's guide (Henshaw)
Motorhomes – A first-time-buyer's guide (Fry)
Pass the MoT test! – How to check & prepare your car for the annual MoT test (Paxton)
Roads with a View – England's greatest views and how to find them by road
    (Corfield)
Roads with a View – Scotland's greatest views and how to find them by road
    (Corfield)
Roads with a View – Wales' greatest views and how to find them by road (Corfield)
Simple fixes for your car – How to do small jobs for yourself and save money (Collins)
Selling your car – How to make your car look great and how to sell it fast (Knight)
The Efficient Driver's Handbook – Your guide to fuel efficient driving techniques and car choice (Moss)
Walking the dog – Motorway walks for drivers and dogs (Rees)
Walking the dog in France – Motorway walks for drivers and dogs (Rees)

www.rac.co.uk
www.veloce.co.uk

This publication has been produced on behalf of RAC by Veloce Publishing Ltd.
The views and the opinions expressed by the author are entirely his own, and
do not necessarily reflect those of RAC. **Please do not undertake any of the
procedures described in this book unless you feel competent to do so,
having first read the full instructions.**

First published in July 2012 by Veloce Publishing Limited, Veloce House,
Parkway Farm Business Park, Middle Farm Way, Poundbury, Dorchester, Dorset,
DT1 3AR, England. ISBN: 978-1-845844-74-5 UPC: 6-36847-04474-9

Fax 01305 250479/e-mail info@veloce.co.uk
web www.veloce.co.uk or www.velocebooks.com.

Pass the MoT test!

How to check & prepare your car for the annual MoT test

Mark Paxton

Includes changes to the test introduced January 2012

Contents

Contents

Introduction

A brief history

With the Second World War finally over, Britain's car factories turned their attention once more to fulfilling the escalating demand for personal mobility. Unfortunately, the country teetered on the edge of bankruptcy, so the shiny new models which rolled off the production line drove straight on to ships for export to the far flung corners of a crumbling Empire, leaving our roads cluttered with a motley collection of prewar vehicles. Poorly maintained, these old bangers soldiered on through the 1950s leaving an escalating accident rate in their smoky wake, which resulted in the Ministry of Transport introducing a basic roadworthiness test in 1960 to check steering, brakes and lights. It applied to all vehicles over ten years old.

This department's initiative not only bequeathed its name to the process, the MoT test for short, but ensured that the public was made aware of the good sense in formulating a compulsory inspection system overseen by the government to ensure public safety. Having achieved that necessary support, its scope grew rapidly. By 1967, the test applied to all cars over three years old, followed a year later by the introduction of tyre checks and a minimum tread depth.

Rising traffic volumes and a corresponding increase in accident rates provided the impetus for yet further action, so, in 1978, body structure checks were introduced to the test, along with exhaust, indicator, wipers, washers and horn inspection. Another flurry of activity in the early 1990s saw the arrival of emissions testing, even tougher tyre regulations, and a plethora of minor inclusions, such as numberplates, rear view mirrors, and fog lamps. In 2005, the whole procedure was computerised, which allowed easier compilation of statistics and integration into other systems,

Checking the car before the MoT test can be a real moneysaver, and lots of the checks are very simple and straightforward.

owners who sometimes view it as an alienating and expensive affair that is entirely out of their control, but it should also be borne in mind that it is a process designed to ensure minimum standards for safe operation of any vehicle used on the road, and as such should be welcomed. The checks carried out are actually quite easy to replicate, and are explained here in a sequence that stretches from the quick and easy to the slightly harder and then on to the most definitely grubbier. Some of the actual test relies on a degree of judgement and discretion on the part of the person carrying out the checks; for example, deciding whether wear in a component is enough to result in failure, so grey areas will always be present, but this volume can at least show the more clear-cut failure points so that they can be eliminated before the big day. VOSA relies on the accumulated experience and judgement of the tester to make the right call. The main considerations that should be taken in to account are:

• " ... whether the component has reached the stage where it is obviously likely to affect adversely the roadworthiness of the vehicle ..."
• " ... whether the condition of the component has clearly reached the stage when replacement, repair or adjustment is necessary ..."

Assuming that the average owner does not have that same level of experience, it is recommended that they should err on the side of caution when carrying out any pre-test checks. A second opinion can always be sought if the component is sufficiently expensive to deter automatic renewal.

The book deals exclusively with the Class 4 test for private cars, and is aimed at vehicles built in the last fifteen years or so. As a result, items

such as the road fund licence scheme (road tax) allowing owners to complete transactions entirely online.

The testing scheme today is controlled by VOSA (Vehicle and Operator Services Agency) which trains and approves testers, issues regulations for the premises used for the test, suitable equipment and its upkeep, and offers a complaints and disciplinary procedure.

Using this book
The MoT test is often dreaded by car

such as separate chassis, king pins, and semaphore indicators have been ignored, as vehicles fitted with these items are very much in the classic field today. Some of the more recent technical developments are commonly known by their acronyms. These are referred to in the main text and, where appropriate, a short definition and description of their purpose is included in Appendix 1.

As this book was being put together the test was being altered once again with effect from January 2012, these changes are included, however their impact cannot yet be assessed.

Acknowledgements

My thanks must go to Luke Bigwood, Press Officer at VOSA for allowing the use of diagrams originally published in the MoT Inspection Manual, and to his colleagues who proof read the main chapters to check that I had interpreted the regulations correctly.

one
Simple checks

The following checks can be made very easily and quickly by even the most inexperienced of owners. Despite that simplicity, though, these items still make up around 30 per cent of faults logged with VOSA on cars which have failed the annual test, so taking the time to check them is very worthwhile.

VIN
All cars built after 1st August 1980 will be subject to a Vehicle Identification Number check. VINs are usually stamped into the bodywork under the bonnet, in the floor next to a sill, or they may be on a plate under the bonnet. There may be more than one VIN plate mounted on the vehicle, but either

All cars have at least one VIN plate. Check that the numbers are legible and the plate secure.

This plate has delaminated and suffered from water intrusion and subsequent staining. As the damage has reached the numbers and letters the vehicle will fail the test.

way, the number must be clear and untampered with.

Numberplates

Numberplates must be present, secure, and the correct colour for their position; which is white with black letters/digits on the front, and yellow with black on the rear if the vehicle was manufactured after January 1973. The backgrounds must be plain, although 3D style numbers/letters with grey edging are acceptable. Cracks, de-lamination, or fading, may all be reasons for failure, as will the plates being too dirty, as they must be fully legible from around 20 metres. The spacing of the numbers and letters will also be checked, as will their style, so attempts at personalisation will fail. The exact dimensions and acceptable fonts can be found in the *MoT Inspection Manual*.

Lights/reflectors

It's possible to have an MoT for vehicles that are exclusively used during daylight hours and not used in reduced visibility, but very few people are likely to want

to take advantage of that particular regulation. If you should happen to be one of them, there must either be no lights fitted or, if there are any, then they have to be permanently disconnected, masked out, or painted over.

Sidelights (front)

For most vehicles, a functioning lighting system is a pretty basic requirement, so the first lamps to be examined are the sidelights (sometimes referred to as daytime running lights).

There must be four lamps, one on each side front and rear, and they cannot be obscured by bodywork or any addition to the vehicle. They have to operate from a switch, the presence of which will be checked. This has to be in reach of the driving position, secure and functioning correctly. Once the lights are turned on, they must light together without excessive delay, and show white light to the front (although a blue tinge is acceptable), and red to the rear. Yellow is also allowed as long as the sidelight is part of a yellow headlight. Their operation must not be compromised by the use of any other lamp. Surprisingly, damage to the lamps is not an automatic fail (it has to be excessive, which is defined as enough to make them not visible at a reasonable distance).

The exact location of the lamps is governed by the Road Vehicle Lighting Regulations and is not covered by the test, though a visual check will be made to ensure that all the lamps are roughly at the same height and distance from each other.

Headlights

Just like the sidelights the headlights have to match, in terms of position, size and light output, and this applies whether there are two lamp units or four. The tester will make sure that they are securely mounted to the body (and you can check this yourself by placing a hand across the glass and gently pushing left and right, then up and down). Those headlights with an adjustment facility inside the car may be spring loaded, but the slight movement from this type of fitting will not result in failure.

The headlight glass, which may be plastic on many modern vehicles, can be failed on anything which alters the pattern of the light passing through it, so cracks, holes, or even heavy scratching on plastic versions, could be problematic. The same criteria applies to the internal surfaces of the unit – rust or de-lamination of the silvering can affect the pattern, and could, therefore, result in a test fail.

The headlight operating switch inside the car must be positive in its action – having to jiggle it to get the lights to work is a failure point. There must be an operational main beam indicator light visible from the driver's seat. The lights must switch between main and dip settings promptly, not leaving both on at any time.

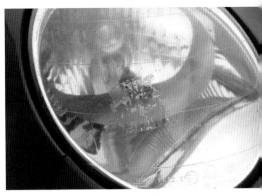

This headlamp has some residue from a beam bender used for a continental trip. Clean off anything that could possibly interfere with the beam pattern.

If the vehicle has HID headlamps they may have a levelling and cleaning system; this will be checked for operation and efficiency. This will also apply to a vehicle with an aftermarket HID system fitted. If there's any doubt as to whether the self-levelling system is working, the client will get the benefit of the doubt and the car will be passed.

Headlight aim

The MoT test station will have a dedicated beam checker, which also allows the aim and pattern of the headlights to be examined closely. At home this can only be roughly checked by measuring the height of the centre of your headlamps and their distance apart, then marking a wall to match. Park the car about six feet away from the wall and turn on main beam (this is best done when natural light levels are low for maximum contrast). The main intensity of each beam should be on the marks that were made, or just below the centre point as measured. Select dip position and the beam should drop to the left-hand side, but remain symmetrical. Any discrepancies between the light cast by the two

The testing station will be equipped with an accurate beam testing machine, the latest versions, such as this one, use lasers to align the headlamp.

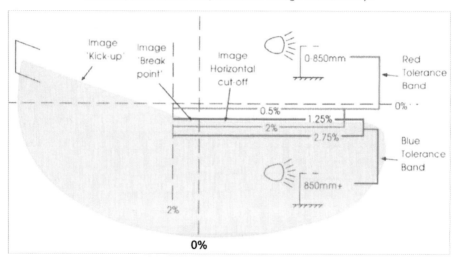

The *VOSA Inspection Manual* sets out different patterns depending on the car's origins. Obviously, there's no way this check can be made at home, but basic alignment certainly can. (Courtesy VOSA)

beams must be rectified. Adjustments can usually be achieved using the screwed rods at the rear of the lamp, with the light still shining on the wall as a guide (you might chose to leave such adjustments to professionals before the car is submitted for its MoT). A common fault is a vague, soft-edged output, which is usually caused by the bulb being incorrectly fitted in its holder, so remove it and check. If you own a car with hydro-pneumatic suspension, the light test will be carried out with the engine running so you

Measure from the ground up to the centre point of the bulb, which should be visible through the glass.

With dipped beam selected, see if the pattern looks like the one in the diagram on page 12. If not, try re-seating the bulb. Make sure that the main intensity of the light is below the bulb height you measured earlier.

must check them at home in the same manner.

If the car has an internal headlight height adjuster, the tester will leave it

If the patten is indistinct, or differs noticeably from one side to the other, it's probably due to an incorrectly seated bulb. Access to change them can be awkward on some recent models.

as it is unless the car is going to fail for the aim being too low, in which case the highest position will be selected and the aim re-checked. If a left-hand drive car is submitted for testing, a headlamp mask or diverter is not an automatic fail, as long as it doesn't significantly reduce light output and the rest of the aim and pattern are passable.

The *MoT Inspection Manual* includes clear colour diagrams, a full list of each type of beam, the regulations covering it, and reasons for failure if you wish to check for further details. Repairs to any part of the vehicle are not allowed during the test, but many stations will make minor adjustments to the beam aim if it's only slightly out of position; this is permitted by VOSA.

Stop and tail lights
First of all, position and symmetry will be visually checked as per the front lights; there must be two stop lights for vehicles used after January 1971. Condition inspection starts with the security of the mountings. Lens cracks which allow white light to escape to the rear will be a fail, as will excessive fading. Brake lights must illuminate and extinguish when the pedal is applied and released.

Using the same wall as the headlight test outlined above, reverse the car up to it and, with the ignition on, press the brake pedal. The stop lights should work immediately and extinguish as soon as the pedal is released. Both units should be of equal brightness. A single non-functioning light is probably down to a blown bulb; both (or all three) failing to work may be due to a faulty switch, but check the bulbs first as they're easier to get at.

Now turn on the sidelights and press the brake pedal again, both circuits should work and remain unaffected by the other. Next, try the indicators on one side; again there should be no interference to the operation of any circuit. If the light units have a bad earth you may find that they dim or flash feebly when more than one circuit is activated. Clean and lubricate all the connections on the light unit and re-try.

If additional stop lights are fitted then they must function. If the tester cannot tell if they are connected, then the benefit of the doubt goes to the owner.

Numberplate light
The first check will be that these lights are actually present, illuminate the plate, and are secure. They must come on with the sidelights and, if there's more than one fitted, all must work. They must adequately illuminate the plate but not show white light directly to the rear. Blown bulbs and corrosion to the lamp terminals are the most common reasons for these lights to fail.

Rear reflectors
There should be two red reflectors, one on each side, securely mounted symmetrically facing to the rear. These are often built in to the light units

Numberplate lights and their fittings often suffer from corrosion, and need a clean up as well as a new bulb.

Rear reflectors are usually built in to the lamp assembly. If you've fitted aftermarket versions, make sure that they include the reflectors.

themselves. They must be securely fitted, and must not be excessively damaged. Reflective tape is not an acceptable substitute.

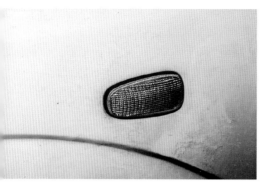

Side repeater lamps are also prone to problems; make sure they work reliably.

Indicators and hazard lights

Just like all the other lights looked at so far, the tester will be checking for secure mounting, lens condition, and proper function. Vehicles used after April 1986 will also be examined for the presence and operation of side-mounted repeater units. These may be separate or built into the main lamp body – if the latter, it

should have an E (or e) mark under the number '5' moulded into the lens. The light emitted from the indicators must be amber, either from the lens itself or from yellow coloured bulbs, fading of either type will result in failure. The indicator switch must be positive in action and undamaged. With the indicators turned on, check that there is a telltale light on the dash, or an audible warning, and that they are working; either is acceptable.

The lights themselves have to flash between 60 and 120 times a minute. If they're slow, the engine can be started and the revs raised slightly above idle to achieve the minimum figure. If they still remain slow, a replacement flasher relay should sort it out. They must not be compromised in any way by the operation of another light circuit (which you will have checked already with the wall test outlined previously).

If your car was used after April

Hazard warning light switches are prone to sticking; turn them on and off a few times and make sure the indicators work as normal afterwards.

1986 there must also be a functioning hazard circuit fitted. Turn on the switch (and only one is permitted) and check that the dash telltale works and all the indicators flash in unison, regardless of whether the ignition is on or off. It's not uncommon for hazard switches to 'stick' as most people use them very infrequently, so it would be wise to operate the switch a few times before the test to ensure that it turns on and off properly. Check, too, that the indicator circuit reverts to its normal state afterwards. A little lubrication will usually alleviate any reluctance at the switch.

Rear foglight
On vehicles used after April 1980, there must be a rear foglight fitted to the centre or nearside of the vehicle. It must have a red lens and a telltale light inside the car. It, too, must not be adversely affected by the use of any other light circuit. To test it, turn on the ignition, select dipped beam, then switch on the foglight switch; the lamp itself should turn on at the back of the car along with the warning light on the dash. Lenses, etc, will be checked as per all the other lights.

Light repairs
Any product that is used on the lenses or light sources (bulbs), which obviously reduces their efficiency or alters the colour of the light emitted, will be a failure. This may impact on the use of commercially available lens repair tapes and similar products, although, once again, tester discretion is used in coming to a judgement. To eliminate any possibility of a fail, it's better to replace any damaged units before the test.

Windscreen
The main checks on the windscreen are for damage, most likely a chip or crack. There are two areas of concern, the section swept by the wipers during

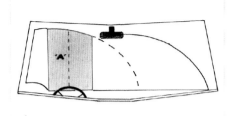

The critical areas of the screen are clearly shown in this diagram. (Courtesy VOSA)

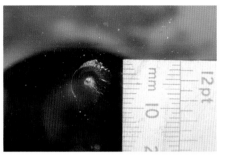

Chips like this should be repaired as a matter of urgency. In the UK at least, this chip is verging on the legal limit of 10mm.

normal use, and a smaller area in front of the driver (290mm wide and centred on the steering wheel 'A'). Any damage in this latter section must be able to be contained within a 10mm diameter circle to pass; in the larger swept area a diameter of 40mm applies. Many commercial windscreen firms offer chemical injections to repair damaged areas, which is accepted for the MoT. Check if the screen can be adequately repaired and if it can be carried out free under the terms of your motor insurance; it often can be. Anything attached to the inside of the screen that seriously obstructs the driver's view will also result in failure.

If a satnav is fitted, it's best to take it and its mount out before the test (it can be removed by the tester at his/her discretion if it's going to result in a

Mirrors must be secure and give an adequate view to the rear.

fail for obstructing the driver's view, but he/she's not obliged to do that, so why take the risk?). Heavy scratching to the screen, from a defective wiper blade, for example, will also be a failure point, but again the extent of that damage is another discretionary point. Minor scratching can often be polished out before the test.

If the car has sun visors which will not remain in the 'up' position, that, too, will result in a fail.

Mirrors
If your vehicle was first used after 1st August 1978, then it must be fitted with at least two mirrors. One must be a driver's side exterior, the other can either be the interior type or another external mirror on the passenger side. All must be secure, and any damage to the glass must not seriously impair the view to the rear. This, again, allows discretion on the part of the tester, so, to be on the safe side, replace any cracked or cloudy glass before the test. There are stick-on replacement mirror glasses available for most popular cars, which saves the expense of changing the whole assembly. Mirrors should be visible and adjustable from the driver's seat. If the car is fitted with rear view cameras

instead of mirrors, then the operation of the system will be checked in pretty much the same way, and if the view to the rear is obscured or is unclear then the car will fail the test.

Washers
The operating switch must work, and the pump has to deliver sufficient liquid to clear the screen when used with the wipers. This really throws up two possible problems, lack of volume and washer nozzle aim. The former may be a result of a weakening pump or blocked lines. A blast of compressed air will usually clear the latter. The jet heads on many cars are pivoting metal balls inside a plastic housing so a pin can be used to change their position quite easily. Make sure the washer reservoir is fully topped up ready for the test.

Wiper blades
Wiper blades must clear the screen

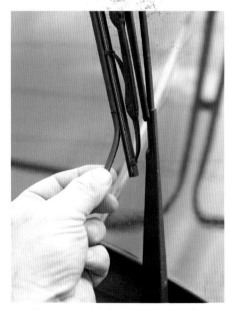

Check wiper blades for splits or other damage.

Dash warning lights will be checked as outlined in the text. Engine management light functions were not included in the test as this book was being produced, however, their addition was considered imminent ...

sufficiently for the driver to have a good view of the road; a condition which theoretically could mean just one wiper working, although it would not be sensible to submit a car in that state so make sure both sides work. Splits to the rubber blades will almost certainly result in failure, so change them if you're in any doubt; they're inexpensive. Check that the blades are secure on the arms, and the arms themselves are tight on their spindles. If the self park is not working it may be a problem if the arms stop in the middle of the screen and the tester decides it interferes with the driver's view of the road.

Horn
The switch will be checked for presence, its position relative to the driver, and then its operation. The noise emitted must be loud enough to warn other users of your presence, and must be one continuous note; it cannot be a bell, gong or siren. Two- or multiple-tone versions will fail if fitted to a car registered after the 1st August 1973.

Strangely, there's also the option to fail the vehicle if the note is 'harsh or grating,' which is, of course, going to be a pretty subjective judgement.

Dash lights
Dashboard warning lights have recently been incorporated as part of the test, so they will be checked; first of all with the ignition turned on for their presence, and then once again with the engine running to make sure that they extinguish correctly and are not indicating a fault in that system. Checks will be made on the headlight main beam, power steering, brake fluid level, tyre pressure, air bag, traction control, ABS and seatbelt warning lights, where fitted. Please refer to Appendix 1 for more information on some of these systems.

Speedometer
One has to be present, compete and not obviously damaged or inoperative. A crack in the glass (plastic) over the dial may be acceptable, as long as the

Tyre tread depth is measured across the centre three-quarters, around the entire circumference. (Courtesy VOSA)

Many manufacturers include depth warning bars in their tread pattern to help drivers gauge the legal minimum.

to maintain them to a higher standard than the minimum set out in the test. The first check is that the tyres match on the same axle. The size is clearly moulded into the sidewall of each tyre, and will read something along the lines of 165/65 R 14. The first two numbers separated by the forward slash provide the 'aspect ratio' of the tyre, differences in either number on tyres fitted to one axle will be a failure, so check they match side-to-side. On most cars all four will be the same, though some may differ front-to-rear. Radial and crossply tyres cannot be mixed on the same axle, and you cannot have crossplys on the rear and radials on the front, although it's rare nowadays to find anything other than radial tyres fitted to a car.

The tyre will be checked for condition – cracks, cuts or bulges in the sidewalls can result in a test fail if the structure of the tyre has been compromised. For most owners, though, a tyre change is the best option if you're in any doubt over such a safety critical component. The tread must be at least 1.6mm deep across the middle three quarters of the tyre width, all the way round. Most treads have wear block indicators moulded in to help with checking the depth. Amazingly, the tread outside the testable area can be bald and still pass, again a sensible owner will replace the tyre and investigate and rectify the cause of the uneven wear.

Cuts to the tyre will result in a fail if they are more than 25mm long or expose any part of the tyre's inner structure; whether cords or steel. A visual check is also made on the rim joint to ensure that the tyre is correctly fitted, that the valve stem is examined for damage and position, and finally that there are no signs that the tyre is making contact with another part

speedo itself is still fully legible, there's no possibility of the needle catching on the damage, and there are no safety issues arising from it. The unit must illuminate when the lighting circuits are operational.

Air bags
If the car was originally fitted with an air bag (or bags), then they must still be present and not obviously defective.

Tyres and rims
As the only contact point with the road, the condition of your tyres is paramount, and, as such, most owners will want

Dented wheel rims may also result in a fail, depending on the severity of the damage.

Missing wheel nuts are a failure point.

This wheel also has a missing nut, but the centre was normally covered by a decorative finishing cap. The test does not include removing trim to check, so this car would have passed.

of the car, be it mechanical or body. Markings such as 'Not For Road Use,' or any incorrectly placed manufacturers' fitting indicators, for example, a sidewall marked 'outer' found on the inside of the wheel will be a fail.

The spare wheel will not be tested, but if it's noticed that there's a problem with it, then the owner should be informed.

The rims must not be dented, and the wheels will be spun to make sure that they are not noticeably out of round. They will also be checked for any signs of cracking, splitting, or other serious damage. Steel rims can have any small dents knocked out with a hammer, though damaged alloys will need to be replaced or repaired by a specialist. The wheel must be securely attached and seated positively to the hub; any elongated mounting holes will result in a fail. Missing wheel nuts or studs are also a fail, but the tester will not remove caps or trim to check.

Do not submit a car with a space saver rim fitted; it will automatically fail. Repair or replace the damaged rim before presenting the car for the test. Finally, if you have a 4x4 or any other vehicle with an externally-mounted spare wheel, then it will be checked for security.

Tow bars

Tow bars will be examined for wear, damage or corrosion to the bar itself and any associated mounts, including fittings (even R pins on detachable versions). Anything deemed to be impairing the safe use of the tow bar will result in a test fail. With detachable types, the mounts will still be checked even if the ball itself is not present.

Towbars will be checked for security and/or any sign of excessive corrosion or damage. Electrical sockets can be failed for damage, a bent mounting like this one will probably not fail, but don't take the chance; address obvious damage like this before submitting the car for the test.

two

A bit more effort

The next batch of items are slightly more time-consuming to examine, but they are well within the capabilities of most owners.

Steering system (internal)

Start off by making sure that the steering wheel itself is in sound condition, any deep cracks or chunks missing from the main covering of the wheel, not just its surface, may result in a test fail if the damage is bad enough to catch the driver's hand and impair movement as the wheel is fed through it. If a metal-spoked wheel is fitted, check the joints to the rim for any signs of damage. Aftermarket and non-standard steering wheels will be assessed in exactly the same manner.

Next, make sure the steering column is locked in place (if it's of the adjustable type). If it will not lock in place then that will be a reason for failure. Grasp the wheel top and bottom and rock it relative to the steering

Grasp the steering wheel top and bottom and rock it (not turn it) to check for play in the column bushes.

column, there is no need to exert very much pressure as play should show up quite easily (take extra care if the car has a collapsible steering column). Make sure that any movement found is not caused by a loose or damaged

Holding the wheel at each side, try to pull it up and down, to check for movement.

column mounting rather than wear in the column bushes.

Hold the wheel at both sides and try to pull it away from the column towards you, any lift will probably point to a loose clamp at the rack, or wear in the lower column joint. Have a look at the lower coupling and check for signs of wear. Move the steering wheel with one hand whilst grasping the joint with the other, and look for movement in the universal joint pins. Check that the pinch bolt is tight, and that there's no play in the splined joint to the rack. Some cars will have a rubber doughnut at the bottom of the column; check it for cracks and splitting. As all this will involve crawling around in the footwell it may be useful to arm yourself with a torch.

Check the amount of free play at the wheel rim, with the road wheels in the straight ahead position. With a rack and pinion steering setup, which is pretty much fitted to all modern cars, there should be virtually no free movement before the road wheels start to turn. The tester will allow up to 13mm before any movement is deemed excessive; however, in reality, there should be considerably less. If the car

Rock the wheel right and left to feel for free movement before the road wheels start to turn.

The testing station will have swivel plates which allow the steering to move from side-to-side with the car's weight on the wheels.

is fitted with power steering the free play must be checked with the engine running. If it is a vehicle with a steering box, the free play allowance is increased to 75mm (see the next chapter for the reasoning behind this).

The test also checks the steering through its full movement for any tight or loose spots in the rack. At the testing station this is done with the weight of the car resting on steel pivot plates, which is impossible for an enthusiast to replicate at home, but slowly moving the steering through its full arc with the wheels on the ground will probably show up any defects. This process can be very hard work on some cars though, so if the effort needed is excessive don't force things, a reasonable assessment can still be made when the vehicle is jacked up.

The last check is on the steering lock mechanism, which, if one was fitted as standard on cars first used after September 2001 (which is pretty much all of them), must be present, securely mounted, and operational. It

The operation of the steering lock will also be checked.

will be checked by turning the wheel through its complete arc with the engine running, if the lock engages it will obviously be a fail. If an electronic steering lock is fitted, the system will fail if the dash warning light is illuminated.

Foot brake system (internal)

All the internal checks revolve around the brake pedal. It must be in sound condition, and be free from damage or excessive corrosion. Grasp the pedal and push and pull it from side-to-side to check its mounts. Have a look at the joints to any rods and linkages and check them for movement including the security of any locking devices fitted such as split or R pins. Make sure that the bodywork around the pedal mounts is not excessively corroded. Have a look too for any signs of hydraulic fluid leaking inside the car which will normally find its way inside along the operating rod which connects to the master cylinder under the bonnet. The pedal rubber must be present, secure and not worn smooth.

Once satisfied with the condition of the pedal, its travel should be assessed. Press the pedal hard to fully operate the brakes (it should stop well before it reaches the floor). If it doesn't and it sinks too far it will be deemed to have insufficient reserve travel to be safe, and the car will fail the test. If the car has drum brakes (found only on the rear wheels on modern cars) adjusting them or replacing the shoes if they are worn out may eliminate the problem. If it doesn't or if the pedal feels spongy rather than firm, then there may be air in the system. If work has recently been carried out on the hydraulics, then bleeding the brake lines may suffice. If not, then the system will need to be checked for leaks. 'Sponginess' without a low pedal need not be a problem, as pedal feel does vary between models and manufacturers.

If a brake servo is fitted, pump the brake pedal a couple of times to exhaust it, then apply firm, continuous pressure to the pedal. With that force maintained, turn on the engine. Once the engine is running, the pedal should almost instantly drop very slightly. If the feel of the pedal is unaltered then the servo is probably not working.

A final check is to very slowly and

The brake pedal will be examined for security, and for wear to the rubber pad.

The amount of travel before the pedal is firm will be assessed.

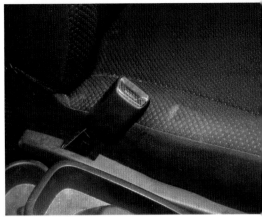

Seats will be checked for security; this will be even more rigorous if the seatbelts are mounted to them.

gently press down on the brake pedal. If the master cylinder is faulty the pedal will sink all the way to the floor. Confirm it by releasing and pressing the pedal quickly. If it instantly feels normal again the master cylinder needs replacing.

If the car has ABS fitted, the warning light will be checked as stated before. Not all systems work in the same way so refer to your vehicle's handbook or manual. Check the sequence required for the light to extinguish and stay out.

Seats

All seats must be securely mounted, which can be checked by rocking them backwards and forwards and side-to-side, and looking for movement. There will inevitably be some movement so the amount has to be deemed sufficient to significantly reduce their security; another area of tester discretion. If they feel loose and clunky, then it will probably be deemed excessive, so investigate where the play lies. Cracking of the seat frame is not uncommon on many models. The seat backs must also be secure when in the normal upright position required when driving. There

will also be a check on fore and aft movement of the seat on its runners, to ensure that at least two positions can be selected. If the seat relies on electric motors for this function then they must work correctly as well.

Doors

All the doors must close and latch securely. The front pair have to be capable of being opened from the inside as well as the outside, the rears just the outside. The doors must open and shut easily without requiring undue force, and

Doors must open using the correct handles, anything else will not pass.

all the hinges, latches and their mounts on the door pillars will be checked for condition. Boot lids and tailgates also have to close securely.

Seatbelts

The regulations governing the types of seatbelts and fittings is quite long, and so this section assumes that a modern car is being dealt with (having three-point belts fitted to the front, and lap/three-point in the rear.

The main area of concern is the condition of the belts and their mounting points. The whole of the belt webbing must be checked, so if the car has inertia reel belts (which is pretty much all of them nowadays), pull the belt out from the reel. Look for splits, fraying edges or even holes where the door may have been inadvertently closed on it. If the lower, inner mount is a stalk, check it for damage, and wiggle it about as the internal strands may be splitting under the plastic sleeve which usually

covers them. Click the seatbelt into place and check that it stays together, pulling on the belt to double-check, then make sure that the release button/clip is not broken, and that it does its job properly. Re-attach the belt and pull it to check the security of the mounting points under strain. Finish off by checking those mounts closely for any damage or corrosion within 30cm of them, although that may be difficult in a modern, carpeted, car, so the examination will have to take place from underneath later on. If the seatbelt is attached to a seat frame rather than a separate stalk, then the condition and mounts of the seat will checked even more closely for defects or corrosion. Finally, ensure that the belt retracts properly into its reel. Minor assistance is acceptable, but it must mainly work under its own steam or it will fail.

If the seatbelt has a pre-tensioner system fitted from new, it must still be present and not have been deployed.

Check all the seatbelt webbing for fraying, holes, or other damage.

Make sure that the seatbelts clip into place.
Give each belt a good tug to make sure.

Bonnet

Like the other closures the bonnet must
latch securely in the closed position.
The device which locks it in place will
also be checked for signs of damage,
deterioration, and security.

Check the handbrake has some reserve
travel left when fully on.

The latch mechanism must secure the
bonnet properly.

Handbrake condition and travel

The lever and button of the handbrake
must be free from damage and securely
mounted. If the floor around the mount
is visible from inside the car it needs
to be checked for rust or cracking
within 30cm. Securing nuts or bolts
also need to be sound and tight. With
the handbrake fully on, try pulling it
upwards away from the floor to feel for
any movement. The lever should also

Try knocking the lever to make sure that it
doesn't release due to worn ratchet teeth.

be wiggled about whilst disengaged to
check for excessive slack in the pivot.

Pull it up one click at a time to check each part of the ratchet mechanism. The brake must be fully operational before the lever runs out of travel, aim for that to happen about mid-way through its potential arc; any more may be regarded as excessive by some testers. With the brake fully on, tap the lever downwards with the heel of your hand to check that it does not disengage, then try once more from each side. If it does disengage, the ratchet teeth and/or pivots are worn and the assembly has to be replaced.

If your car is fitted with an electronic parking brake then, with the handbrake off, an illuminated warning light on the dash will result in a test fail, as will any modification or repair that the tester decides has been inappropriately or inadequately made to any of the controls.

External bodywork

The main check here is for projecting sharp edges caused either through

Corroded bodywork will not necessarily result in a fail, but if it's holed it could be deemed dangerous and then it will.

Accident damage is not an automatic fail, but if the door edge here was bent any further out then, once again, it could be considered dangerous.

impact damage or by corrosion. Once again this entails a degree of tester discretion, so to be on the safe side treat any jagged edge as a fail point, and rectify the issue before submitting the car. Bumper edges and trim, the front of the bonnet and wings and door bottoms are likely to attract the most attention.

Under-bonnet checks (general)
Master cylinder
The brake fluid level will be checked if visible through the bottle, so if this is dirty clean it and make sure the fluid level is correct. The master cylinder will be checked for leaks (usually at the joints to the brake lines or to the servo, where fitted). The lines around the engine bay will be examined for security, damage and corrosion.

Master cylinders can leak where the bottle is attached (left arrow), and out of the rear seal where it meets the servo (right arrow). Check the pipe unions as well.

Make sure that the brake fluid reservoir is topped up with the correct fluid and not leaking.

Battery security and the condition of the wiring is also part of the test now. Make sure it is all clean and tidy.

Battery and wiring

The condition and attachment of the battery will be assessed. If it is insecure or there are signs of leaking electrolyte, it will fail. If the terminals are crusty/ corroded, it would be advisable to clean them (by pouring very hot water on them), then dry and grease them.

All electrical wiring will be examined for security and support, so there can be no chance of accidental damage. If any has occurred and there are any bare wires or connectors showing, it will result in a fail. 7- and 13-pin trailer sockets are also checked for security and damage, including whether a lead can be safely mounted. They will be checked even if the towbar is removed (detachable types) but the mountings are still present. 13-pin sockets will also be checked for electrical operation, and a device will be attached to ensure that everything is wired correctly to illuminate the foglamp, indicators, position, and stop lamps.

Power steering

The power steering bottle will be inspected for security, and all unions and pipework will be examined for leaks. The level fluid is checked, so it would be foolish to take the car without checking that it's topped up.

Fuel leaks

Make sure all lines are secure and leak free. There will usually be some telltale staining or smell to indicate a problem. If the car has a gas system (LPG) fitted, a leak check will be carried out using a specific spray. These aerosols can be purchased from any decent motor factors if you wish to check for leaks yourself before the test.

three
Getting dirty

Safety first
This series of checks is best carried out with the vehicle raised and properly supported on axle stands. **Caution!** Make sure the car is completely stable before venturing underneath – this would usually include chocking the non-elevated wheels to prevent any movement. Never use a jack on its own or be tempted by homemade supports, use items designed and sold for the purpose, be they stands or ramps. These must be used on level ground.

A light will be useful when examining the underside, a 12-volt inspection lamp is best (if a mains unit is all that's available, then make sure that an appropriate circuit breaker is incorporated). Some checks need to be done with the engine running, so make sure you're fully aware of all moving components, and that you have no loose clothing or hair which could be caught.

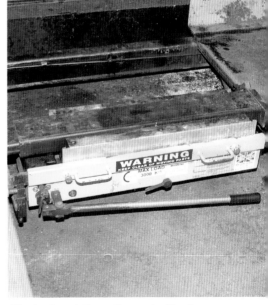

The testing station will use a jacking beam to raise the car. At home a jack and axle stands will have to do, so make sure the car is completely secure when raised.

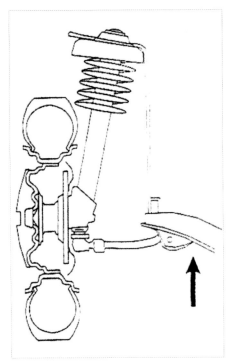

The *Inspection Manual* has several diagrams showing where to jack vehicles depending on the type of suspension fitted. For most modern cars, supporting the body leaving the suspension hanging will be the right solution. (Courtesy VOSA)

The *MoT Inspection Manual* indicates where cars with specific types of suspension have to be jacked up in order to assess wear in suspension components. For most recent vehicles (last 15 years or so), it's fine to support the body leaving the suspension free and under its own weight.

The items in this section are laid out by their function, a small degree of repetition is inevitable, so read through the whole chapter first and then decide which tests can be suitably combined when you're under the car. The checks made here could eliminate a significant amount of defects recorded by VOSA.

Vehicle structure (main sections)

The MoT checks on vehicle structure are dependent on the original design and construction of the car, and whether certain parts (referred to as prescribed areas in the *Inspection Manual*), are load bearing or not. In addition, any area within 30cm of any safety related item will also be checked, plus any part which is deemed to be playing a role in supporting the vehicle as a whole and which is corroded or damaged sufficiently to hinder the safe operation of steering, suspension or brakes.

For the average owner it's easier just to assume that any defect you find will be a failure point, and rectification will have to be undertaken before submitting the car for its test. Excessive corrosion, damage or inadequately carried out repairs are what you are looking for, and make sure to include subframes and crossmembers in your check as well as the main body.

The first structural problem to assess is rust. Surface rust is not a problem, the test looks for items 'corroded to excess.' If rust is found the tester will prod or tap it with a VOSA approved tool; at home a screwdriver will do the job just as well. Obviously, if the metalwork holes under prodding, the vehicle will fail the test; if the tester feels there is too much 'give,' it will fail also. Good steel should be completely firm under pressure and ring cleanly when struck with the screwdriver handle, rotten metal will creak. The tapping test will also be applied to areas where the tester suspects that filler or a similar product has been used to cover up corrosion. Blistered steel can be scraped to see if the scabs fall off leaving holes behind.

If the steel is damaged, either from an accident, an improper modification, or from fatigue, the vehicle will fail the test. Assessing this properly will come

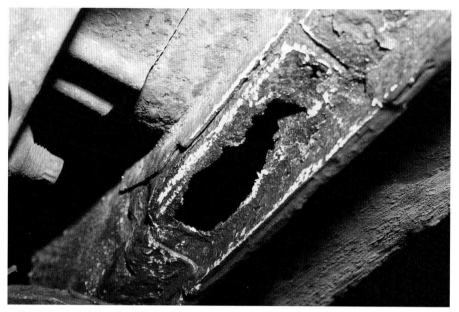

Rust-damaged steel is going to be a problem virtually anywhere on the underside of the car. This inner sill has been marked with yellow crayon (used by many testing stations to highlight the defect).

The front chassis legs on modern vehicles tend to run along the inside of the inner wings; check them carefully for corrosion (engine removed here for clarity).

If a separate subframe is fitted, then make sure the area around the mounts is not suffering from rust, and that bushes and bolts have not deteriorated.

There will be box sections under the floor to strengthen the bodyshell. Again, check for rust or damage which might weaken them.

down to experience, but cracks or tears should be obvious, and any panel joins opening up around their spot welds should be easy to see.

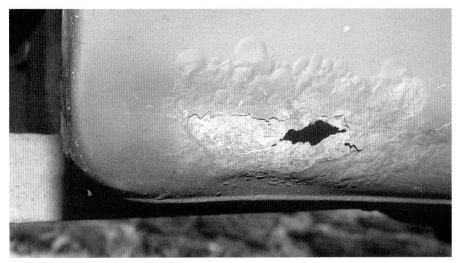

Some corrosion may not fall within the regulations, but it's better to repair it before submitting the car for test.

Wheelarch liners have gone a long way in protecting the steelwork, but they also prevent easy inspection from underneath.

Starting at the front of the car, check the chassis legs – usually found exiting the bulkhead and running along both sides of the engine bay, before joining a front crossmember. Inspect all of these carefully, including any box sections bolted to them. Examine the inner wings (they may not be fully visible as liners are often fitted), especially the metalwork around the top of the suspension struts. If the car relies on a separate subframe then it, too, must be checked for corrosion, or any within 30cm of its mounting points to the main body.

The middle section of the car may have box sections running its full length, but many rely instead on the sill structure for strength in this area. Check the floor, especially around the joints to the inner sills, the inner sills themselves, and also the seatbelt and handbrake mounting points. Floors or outriggers at the very front, where the bulkhead bends upwards, are very prone to attack from road debris, so be especially vigilant around that area. Outer sills can be checked easily – they usually start rotting at the bottom and towards the rear.

At the rear of the vehicle, inspect around suspension mounts, spring hangers, and/or subframe mounts. The boot floor often rusts due to water getting past leaking seals, and the area around the petrol tank suffers if it sits directly in the floor.

The sill structure inside the car needs checking as well; though this area is usually carpeted, so it can only be assessed by squeezing the sill as best you can and listening and feeling for any indication that the metal is rusty and failing. The tester may also knock the sill with his/her hand to detect any change in sound along its length.

Under the bonnet

The main areas to check are the inner wings, especially the area around the front suspension mounting tops. As well as rust, look out for signs of distortion that may indicate corrosion around this critical point. Check out the top surface of the front crossmember under the radiator, if it's visible, as well as its joints to the inner wings. The bulkhead, too, can suffer, due to blocked drain tubes, so pay particular attention around steering or braking component mounting points.

Crossmembers under the radiator are prone to rot, so pay them additional attention.

Check the strut tops (if applicable) from inside the bonnet. Rust here was commonplace on older cars, but improved design means it's much less so today.

Inside the boot

The main areas of concern in the boot are the suspension mounts, the metalwork of the inner wheelarches, and the boot floor, especially at the edges as these are most likely to rust first.

Repairs to the structure

If you find any penetrating rust, or if

Welded repairs must be seam welded (top arrow) unless they're secured at an edge which was originally spot welded (bottom arrow).

you own an old car which already has had some welded repairs, then there are a couple of things to bear in mind. Patch repairs are perfectly acceptable as long as they adequately replace the strength lost through the corrosion, and are welded completely around their circumference (unless they are at a panel edge which was spot welded by the manufacturer originally, in which case stitch welds are acceptable). No other form of repair will pass the test; rivets and/or filler are not permitted.

Steering system (rack and pinion – external)

Start the check under the bonnet. Follow the steering column down and, if possible, examine the coupling or join to the steering rack if it wasn't checked during the internal inspection earlier. Have an assistant rock the steering wheel as you look for free play. If any is visible, check the rack mountings and rubber bushes, where fitted, for security and deterioration.

Grasp one of the road wheels and turn it slowly from lock-to-lock, feeling for tight spots in the mechanism. This check will be done with the car on swivel plates during the MoT, but that's impossible to replicate at home. Make sure that nothing fouls as the wheels are turned, especially brake hoses. If a hose is visibly stretched or kinked the vehicle will fail the test.

Bring the road wheel back to the straight ahead position, then, holding it with your hands in the 'quarter-to-three' position, push and pull the rim in short, firm jerks. This will reveal any play in the trackrod ends. If play is suspected, you can confirm it by peering around the wheel whilst it's on full lock, and watching as you move the rim (alternatively, have an assistant rock it as you watch). Continue this movement but turn your attention to the inner connection to the rack (this will be covered by a rubber boot). Check for any in-and-out play before

Check the steering rack mounts for security, and the bushes for wear.

Make sure that brake hoses aren't snagging on anything as the wheels turn from side-to-side.

Hold the rim at the 'quarter-to-three' position when checking the steering joints.

the rack itself starts to move. The boots must be undamaged and not leaking oil or grease. The steering pinion, which is found where the column joins the rack, is usually supported by a bearing. This bearing can wear with time and mileage, so check that the input shaft (the splined

Steering rack boots must not be split or insecure.

bit where the column is clamped) doesn't float around in relation to the body of the rack. If the dust covers on the trackrod end or the steering rack boots are damaged in any way – so they're no longer able to prevent dirt getting in – then the vehicle will fail the test. These tests will show up most play, but it can be useful to check with the car actually on its wheels, which can be tricky to do at home as access under the car can be limited.

If a steering damper is fitted then it must be secure and not leaking. The area of the body within 30cm of any steering mountings will be checked for rust or distortion.

Power steering

The checks listed above for manual steering are all carried out, plus some additional ones. The power steering fluid must be above the minimum level marked on the reservoir; this is a visual check only. The pipes and hoses must be not be excessively corroded or damaged, and must not foul on

any other part of the car. The lock-to-lock test will be done with the engine running, and the tester will assess if the system is working through the full range of movement. The assembly will then be checked for leaks. The power steering ram and its housing must not be damaged, and there must not be excessive play at the anchorage point. If free play is found at the ram ball pin, the tester can check it again with the engine off by applying manual leverage to assess it for movement.

The power steering pump and its drivebelt will be checked, as far as possible, for condition and security, and for any repairs and modifications that may have been carried out. If the system has been disconnected or removed when it was originally part of the car's specifications, that, too, is a fail. If it was an option originally and it has subsequently been disconnected, then the tester can drive the car and decide whether there has been an adverse effect on the steering. If it is decided there has, then that will be a fail.

Top up the power steering reservoir before the car is inspected, and make sure hoses are secure and leak free.

The pump must also be securely mounted, and all the connections free of leaks.

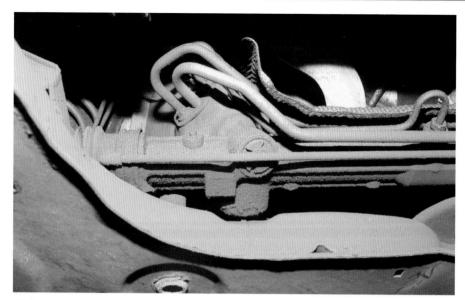

If the rack is covered in oily residue, like this one, clean it off, locate the leak, and rectify it.

Electronic power steering

The same checks are carried out as with manual steering systems, but if the Malfunction Indicator Lamp is illuminated on the dash the car will fail. If there is an Electronic Park Assist button, then failure to activate will not be a problem as long as the rest of the steering system is unaffected. Once again, the tester may elect to fully verify this by a road test.

Electrically-assisted steering will have a malfunction warning light on the dash; make sure that it goes out when the engine is running.

Steering system (steering box external)

If you own a 4x4, the steering system may rely on a box rather than a rack, and this may be manual or have power assistance. The box can be found attached to the inner wing, usually at the end of the steering column. The first test is to check that no movement, or at least only a very small amount, is lost between the steering effort going in, and what comes out of the box. Rock the steering or grasp the column and twist, then watch the drop arm (the lever that exits the box), for an immediate response. A small amount of play is expected on this type of system, but a noticeable lag in movement will result in the vehicle failing the test. Try grabbing the drop arm and pushing and pulling it in relation to the box to feel for any movement.

The drop arm will be connected across the car by a long rod to another box on the other side, once again mounted to the inner wing/chassis. Push and pull it, too. There will be ball joints at each end of this cross-car rod, which must be checked for play or damage to their boots. There will also be further rods connected to the hubs, again, the joints have to be examined closely, including any split pins or locking nuts. All these connections mean that even very small amounts of wear in each part accumulate to give a larger total than with a rack setup, hence the extra free travel (75mm) allowed at the steering wheel for box-equipped vehicles.

To double-check a box system, it may be useful to watch each joint as the steering wheel is rocked with the vehicle back on its wheels, just like for the rack system. How easy this is depends on the amount of space available to view each joint, but on a 4x4 most should still be visible. This is also a good time to check the mountings of the box, and idler mechanism to the body. As strain is put on the steering, check that the box doesn't try to pull away from its mountings (or from the steelwork, in the event of there being corrosion or cracking).

Front and rear suspension

There must be adequate clearance between the suspension and the chassis or any bump stops fitted. If the car has sagged because of weak springs, with the result that part(s) of the body come into contact with the

Check the front coil spring for damage, especially at the ends. Make sure that the damper unit (inside the coils) isn't leaking.

wheel(s) when loaded, then the vehicle will fail the test.

Where the suspension or its mounting system, for example a subframe, meets the body (and within 30cm of that point), look for any corrosion, distortion or fracturing which significantly reduces the original strength of that component. Any previous repairs will also be checked to ensure that they adequately replace that strength.

Front coil springs and their locating seats will be examined for cracking or corrosion. These break with some frequency nowadays, so take the time to check them carefully, as it's not uncommon for a short section at one end to break off. This is a debatable failure point as the regulations state that if the "... extreme end ..." is damaged, then it should only fail if the functioning of the spring is impaired, or if the end doesn't locate properly without assistance when the car is lowered after jacking. Some modern cars have springs which will drop below their bottom mounts when broken, and interfere with the suspension and brake lines when they do, so it's better to replace any spring found to be damaged; they are, after all, safety-related components.

Leaf springs, including their mounting eyes, will be examined for damage. If the leaves are splayed out and the tester decides the action is being impaired, the vehicle will fail the test (the same is true if there's any contact between the leaf and the body). The spring mounting pins will be levered to check movement (this is limited to 2mm for a 12mm pin, and 3mm for a 25mm pin; both of which are pretty small amounts). The eye bush will fail for similar play due to deterioration. Side-to-side movement at the mountings must not exceed 6mm. The mounting plates themselves must be free from

Similar checks apply at the rear of the car. The spring (3), the shock absorber (2) and the brake hose (1).

Check all the hardware associated with the suspension. This trailing arm was split in two, a potentially lethal defect.

On the same car, but on the other side, the trailing arm mounting on the axle has also rusted through.

cracks or other damage including excessive corrosion. Mounting bolts must all be present and tight.

During the suspension check all associated components will be examined, including wishbones,

47

radius arms, subframes, anti-roll bars, etc. All these related parts and their mountings will be checked for missing fittings, wear, rust, or other damage. Mounting bushes and pins will fail if there's sufficient deterioration to allow excessive movement, as will any rubber mounts in the same condition. If any of the components rely on a ball joint for location, then it, too, will fail if excessive movement is found, or if the joint cover is missing or damaged and dirt is able to enter. It's impossible to list here all the various suspension layouts fitted, but the test criteria remains the same for all of them, so make sure anything bolted to the suspension front or back is examined carefully. The vehicle will also fail if a component originally fitted by the manufacturer is removed.

Wheel bearings/suspension joints
The front wheels will be spun initially whilst the tester listens for any noise

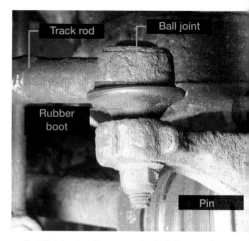

Ball joints develop wear in their internal sockets. This shows up as play between the pin, and the main body of the balljoint socket. A split rubber boot is also a reason for failure.

which may indicate roughness in the bearing. This can be difficult to assess,

Holding the rim at the top and bottom and rocking it will show up wheel bearing and suspension joint wear.

Look for movement (other than swivelling) between the points indicated by the arrows.

The inner end of the suspension arm(s) usually has rubber bushes. Again, make sure that there's no play between the arm and the mounting, which would indicate that the bush was failing.

if you think you can hear any during your pre-test inspection try turning the wheel with just a finger tip, roughness can often be felt as well as heard. Next,

A typical front suspension arm will have this type of set-up. An inner bush, on the left, a ball joint, far right (note the split boot, arrowed), and some form of anti-roll bar connection, in this case rubber bushes, in the middle.

At the rear, check the bushes at all the pivot points, any anti-roll bar bushes, the metalwork itself, and the brake connections.

grasp the wheel and try to rock it. If play is detected, a process of elimination has to be followed to decide where it actually lies. Get an assistant to apply the brakes, if the play disappears, then it's likely to be in the wheel bearing; if it's still there, then it will be in a suspension joint.

If play in the wheel bearings has been eliminated, rock the wheel once more, holding it top and bottom, and check again for play. It may be

This rear trailing arm had its top mount in a rather inaccessible place. It's worth checking, though, as the bush was protruding from the metal pressing, indicating that it had moved and was, therefore, no longer secure.

Anti-roll bar connections to the suspension arms, front or rear, may be by through-bolts (1) and bushes (2). As well as wear to the rubbers, this type often ends up snapping, so make sure that the through-bolt is in one piece.

necessary to turn the rim on to full lock and peer around it to see what's going on. If this proves difficult get someone to rock the wheel for you as you check things out. Look closely at the top and bottom ball joints, and the inner mountings of the wishbone/bottom suspension arm. There may be play at

51

the top of the MacPherson strut (which can have a bearing or a rubber bush), where it meets the inner wing. Some cars have play here when the weight is off the suspension by design, so some homework may be required before condemning these parts.

Now, rock the wheel once again and check the ball joints and inner bushes for play.

Rear wheel bearings can be checked by spinning and listening for roughness, followed by a wheel rock to check for play. Some rear wheel bearings (taper type, not solid) can be re-greased and/or adjusted to eliminate excessive play.

CV joints/boots

The driveshafts themselves will be checked for distortion or damage, turning them fully should show up the former as the shaft will appear to rise and fall; if it's bent the vehicle will

not pass the test. If any shaft passes through a support bearing, which usually means the longer one, grasp the shaft and lift it up and down and look for any signs of play in the bearing or in the housing mountings. Next, move a wheel onto full lock and slowly turn it, checking the pleats of the CV joint

The same applies on the underside. Check the support bearing for the driveshaft (arrowed). Excessive play means the vehicle will fail.

Check CV boots for splitting; there may be telltale smudges of grease. Look for signs of insecurity, such as the shiny section on the joint shown here.

Oil leaks are not themselves an automatic failure point, but long-term they can cause cause problems to rubber components, and, if really heavy, the tester may decline to carry on with the inspection.

boot for damage or insecurity resulting in leaks, then do the same on the other side. Just like the suspension ball joint boots, if dirt can get in then the vehicle will fail. The shaft should be wiggled once more and the CV joint examined for excess play.

Oil leaks

These are not actually a failure point on their own, though if they're heavy some testers may elect not to test the car until the mess is cleaned up, which is inconvenient. Oil leaking onto rubber suspension joints or parts of the braking system is unwelcome at any time. Rectification of the leak should be seen as a priority, as it will cause serious deterioration in rubber components very quickly if left.

Shock absorbers

All shock absorbers regardless of type will be examined for signs of leakage, which must be sufficiently bad to suggest that the seal has failed; a slight misty contamination will not be a reason to fail. Mounting bushes and pins will be checked for deterioration and excessive play. If the suspension unit is rusted to the point where its operation is compromised then it will have to be replaced.

Exhaust system

The exhaust system must be adequately supported – missing mountings don't automatically mean a fail, but it makes sense to submit the car with a full compliment. It will then be inspected with the engine running to make sure that there are no leaks, which will have to be 'major' to fail – a pin hole or leaky clamp should not fail, but a leak may affect the operation of the catalytic converter, so it's best to

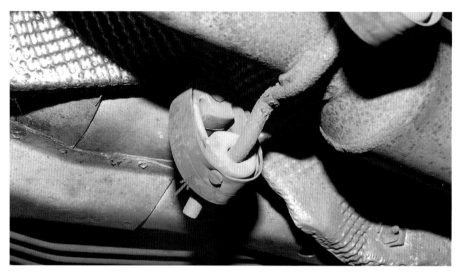

Exhausts must be securely mounted. This one has had an additional rubber ring screwed to the broken original as a repair. This repair passed the test, but another tester may not agree so it would be wise to replace inexpensive items like this before submitting the car.

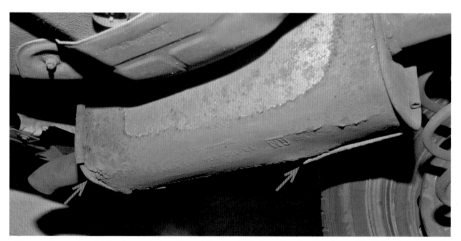

The system should be free of significant leaks. This box is starting to split at the joints, but there's no black staining to suggest gases are escaping so it will pass the test.

eliminate them before submitting the car for the test. Leaks can usually be identified by the telltale black carbon trail at the hole. Repairs are permissible as long as they don't leak, are 'durable,' and the system as a whole remains in a structurally sound condition. Some

exhaust back boxes come from the factory with a small hole drilled at the lowest point to allow accumulated water from condensation to drain away; this will not be a failure point. Exhaust noise is assessed entirely by the tester's ear. If it's deemed to be louder than that normally expected for a similar car in 'average' condition, then the vehicle will fail.

The final check is that the silencer tailpipe is far enough away from the body to prevent fumes entering the interior.

Fuel system
All supply and return pipes will be checked for damage, with and without the engine running. The lines must be properly secured to the body. The filler cap and neck will be examined for split seals or any other damage or

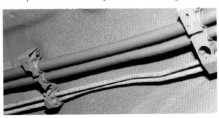

Fuel lines must be free of leaks and mounted securely. The pipes may be plastic or steel.

A missing petrol flap and no cap underneath. There's no point submitting a car without addressing such obvious defects.

All visible parts of the fuel delivery system will be checked. This filter hasn't been changed in a long time, and is very rusty. If there are any signs of leakage however slight then it will fail.

Petrol tanks must be secure and leak-free. Steel tanks are more of a problem than plastic, as they tend to rust at the seams and then weep fuel. Replacement is the only answer.

Engine mounts will be checked, and, if the car is front-wheel drive, then mounts on the gearbox will also be included in the examination. Check the rubber bushes for damage.

deterioration that could result in a fuel leak. The type of cap fitted must also close positively for the same reason, so push-in 'emergency' types will fail. If the petrol pump and/or the fuel filter is visible to the tester they will be checked for leaks and security of mounting. The fuel tank will be checked for corrosion or damage to its mounts, including inside the boot as we have already seen.

Engine mounts

Mounts will be examined for security and signs of excessive movement or deterioration. If one is missing, the vehicle will fail. Front-wheel drive cars which rely on a mount to the gearbox will also have that examined.

Brakes

Starting at the front, the calipers will be checked for leaks, so get an assistant to hold the brake pedal down (or jam it there if you're on your own), and look for signs of fluid loss. Check the flexible brake lines for signs of swelling or bulging. Take the pressure off again, temporarily, and have a look at the discs if they are not shrouded by metal or

Check flexible hoses for cracking. Bending the hose back on itself will show them up more readily.

Pad inspection slot in the rear of the calliper.

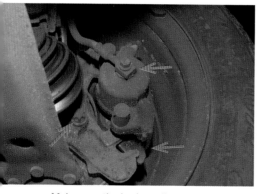

Make sure the brake calipers are secure, that there are no leaks at the brake line unions, and, if the pads are visible, that they have more than 1.5mm of friction material left on them.

plastic splash plates. If they're heavily scored or rust damaged, the vehicle will fail. If the pads can be seen, they will be checked for the amount of wear remaining. If they have less than 1.5mm of friction material left, the vehicle will fail. Mounting bolts and/or securing pins will be checked for presence and security, including locking nuts or pins. Take a second look at the flexible

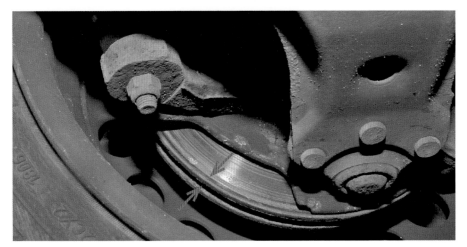

If the discs are visible check them for excessive wear or corrosion. These have a very heavy wear lip at the edge and should be changed as they are likely to fail. It is always better to be cautious with such safety critical components.

hoses, checking for deterioration, cuts, or any other damage. Bending the hose back on itself will show if the rubber is cracking. Make sure that the hose is not kinked, and is attached to its mounts correctly. Obviously, any sign of it contacting the body or wheel will result in a fail.

Move down the underside of the vehicle, checking the metal brake lines for rust or damage. Light surface corrosion shouldn't be a problem, but

Brake lines tend to rust where they bend around the body, and also where they pass through securing clips. Check them very carefully at these points.

if you find some, clean it off and grease the surface to help prevent its return. Apply pressure to the brake again, and check for leaks at all unions. Lines should be securely mounted to the body.

At the rear, if calipers are fitted they will be checked in exactly the same manner as those at the front, including discs and pads. Some cars will have inboard discs at the back, and access may be limited. If drums are fitted, check the brake pipe-to-wheel cylinder join for leaks; staining here will usually give the game away. The tester will also look at the bottom of the plate for any sign of an internal leak, and on rear-wheel drive cars at the point where the axle meets, for leaking oil from faulty seals. The condition of external brake levers and their fittings will also be examined. Rear flexible hoses should be checked for damage and ballooning as before.

Some cars may also have a compensating valve in the rear brake circuit to allow for differences in load.

Brake lines at the back may be better inspected with the wheels off.

If it's connected physically to the rear suspension, with a lever working on an exposed valve to regulate the fluid flow, make sure that it's all free to move and that the valve is not seized. Brake pipe connections should be leak-free.

If a limiting valve is fitted, make sure that the unions are leak-free, and that any mechanical linkages aren't seized. This one has been heavily greased to prevent problems.

four
The hard bits

Emissions

Without the correct gas analysis equipment it's impossible to replicate the test procedure, but there are a few precautions that could prevent a test failure. Make sure that the engine is serviced and tuned correctly, and replace worn sparkplugs and dirty air filters. Check for disconnected vacuum hoses; these can cause havoc out of all proportion to their apparent importance. If the engine management light is on, have the logged codes read and rectify the problem before the test. It's assumed for the purposes of this book that the car was first used after 1st August 1995.

Petrol cars

An initial test is made on visible smoke, and is done once the car has warmed up to its normal operating temperature and is idling at its normal speed. The engine is revved to approximately 2500rpm and held there for 20 seconds

Emissions are impossible to check at home, but to give the car a fighting chance of meeting them make sure the sparkplugs and air filter are in good condition.

to allow the system to purge, then allowed to drop to idle once more. Dense black or blue smoke emitted at idle for more than five seconds is a fail, as is an overly fast idle speed. The engine is then rapidly brought back up to 2500rpm and, if excessive dense blue smoke or clearly visible black smoke is emitted during this burst, and which is likely to obscure the view of other road users, the vehicle will fail. Blue smoke is caused by the engine burning oil, whereas black smoke is due to an overly rich fuel mixture.

With the initial smoke test out of the way, the gas analysis probe will be inserted into the exhaust tailpipe. If specific data for your vehicle is available, then the limits listed are used. If there's no data available, then the default settings listed below are used.

The engine must initially be idling without any additional load, so heated screens, lights, etc, should all be turned off. The tester will raise the idle until the correct operating temperature has been reached – either by relying on judgement or by using a specific probe. A device to accurately read rpm will also be attached. Once satisfied that the car is ready, a 'hang-up check' – to make sure the machine is reading a hydrocarbon level of less than 20 parts per million – is done, then the probe inserted. The analyser will then read the hydrocarbons, with 200ppm being the maximum permitted; carbon monoxide 0.3 per cent maximum (or 0.2 per cent if the car was first used after 1st September 2002); and lambda, between 0.97 to 1.03 allowed; all measured at a fast idle which is maintained for 30 seconds. A second fast idle test is then done, holding the car between 2000 and 3000rpm for three minutes, or until the emissions are within limits. The check is finished by looking at carbon monoxide once again, which must be 0.5 per cent maximum (0.3 after 1/9/2002) at normal idle.

A modern car in good mechanical

```
RPM      ----       2450-3050
NO CHECKED

CO      0.49 %     0.30 MAX
FAIL

HC        82 ppm   200 MAX
PASS

Lambda 1.03      0.97-1.03
PASS

-------------------------
   SECOND FAST IDLE TEST
            PASS
-------------------------
ITEM   ACTUAL      LIMIT

RPM      ----       2450-3050
NO CHECKED

CO      0.16 %     0.30 MAX
PASS

HC        52 ppm   200 MAX
PASS

Lambda 1.00      0.97-1.03
PASS

-------------------------
    NATURAL IDLE TEST
            PASS
-------------------------
ITEM   ACTUAL      LIMIT

RPM      ----        850-1050
NO CHECKED

CO      0.10 %     0.10 MAX
PASS

-------------------------
      OVERALL RESULT
  EXHAUST EMISSION TEST:

          PASSED
-------------------------

-------------------------
TESTED BY:
              ------
```

You will receive a printout of the car's emissions test, whether it passes or fails.

condition will be able to meet these standards quite easily. A print out of the actual recorded figures will be supplied, along with either the pass or fail certificate, and a copy is retained by the testing station for three months.

Diesel cars

Before starting the emissions test on a diesel, the oil level must be checked and the engine at normal operating temperature. The tester will not continue if there is any abnormal engine noise, there is any indication of low oil pressure, or if there is any uncertainty as to the condition of the timing belt.

Cars used after 1st August 1979 will then be tested using a smoke meter with a probe in the exhaust pipe. The engine is purged as per the petrol version, then the meter is zeroed, the probe inserted, and the car restarted. The engine is then quickly revved to its maximum fuel delivery position, the machine indicates when to release the throttle and the revs are allowed to drop back to idle. The smoke meter will then give a reading, $1.50m^{-1}$ being a pass. If the reading is above this, rev outs are permitted to try and bring the reading down and within limits. If it's still is too high, a further three readings can be undertaken. The mean value of these three readings is calculated and, if above 1.50m-1 for cars made after 1st July 2008, the vehicle will fail the test. If the vehicle was made before that date, a non-turbo motor is permitted a maximum of 2.50m-1, a turbo 3.00m-1.

In addition to the metered check, the car will still fail if the tester considers that the density of the smoke emitted is likely to obscure the vision of other road users.

Dual fuel cars

These cars use a combination of LPG and petrol, and can be switched between the two. The tester will leave the vehicle running on whichever fuel it was using when it arrived for the test. The hydrocarbon emissions will be different due to the gases involved, but the station will have a pre-set dividing number to make them comparable.

Brake performance

This part of the test is carried out on brake rollers (some 4x4 vehicles aren't suitable for this test due to their transmission setups, so these will be tested on the road using a decelerometer) and therefore cannot easily be checked by the owner. There are, however, a few things which can be used to get a general indication before the test. If the car has been well maintained, and there are no leaks or damage to any of the brake components, then there should not really be any problems.

Start by applying the handbrake

The official brake test will be done using a dedicated roller; a home check can still give an indication of problems.

The tester will assess braking effort, in this case it is displayed as line of green and red lights. The machine also shows any imbalance in effort as a percentage.

fully, and then select first gear and try to drive away slowly; the rear should dip under the load. If one side drops more notably than the other, then that side is more efficient. The brakes will need to be stripped, cleaned and adjusted, and the test tried again. There may always be a slight difference, but if it's immediately noticeable then there's a problem. To check for a sticking handbrake, roll the car by hand to make sure it moves freely, have an assistant pull hard on the handbrake, and then release it again while you try to roll the

car again. If it's harder to move for the first few revolutions then the handbrake is sticking.

The foot brakes can be checked on an empty piece of level road, ideally somewhere where there no other traffic. **Caution!** Do not carry out the following if you have found defects in the steering or suspension in your checks so far. If everything is in good condition then drive the car very slowly (and 10mph is probably enough), apply the brakes gently, and feel for any tendency for the car to pull to one side. If the road

The best way for most owners to know how well their brakes are going to perform is to strip, clean, and adjust them prior to the test.

is cambered the car will naturally follow that so, for the best results, the road, or even better a large empty car park, must be flat. Try again, this time operating the brakes slightly more firmly (not like in an emergency stop situation), and check that the car pulls up in a straight line to a complete halt. Finally, repeat the last exercise but release the brakes before the car stops, and make sure there is no tendency to veer to one side or the other. If it does, then the brakes are sticking on and not releasing cleanly.

These tests are pretty basic, but can indicate faults which can then be rectified before the car is submitted for the MoT.

five
The big day

Choosing a test station

There are thousands of licensed MoT testing stations in the UK, so unless you live in a particularly remote part of the country there should be plenty of choice. They are clearly identified by the three triangle symbol which will be mounted on the exterior of the building.

VOSA goes to great lengths to ensure that the test procedures are uniformly applied, so there should be no obvious difference between any of them. The best option is probably a personal recommendation. Many people advocate using a testing station that does not do repairs, although the downside of that option is you may end up with additional test fees if the vehicle fails on any items not covered by the free re-test regulations. Your local council will almost certainly have its own testing facilities, and may be a sensible choice. Heavily discounted test fees may appear attractive, but they were originally set to reflect the time needed

It isn't hard finding a testing station, there are thousands around the country.

to carry out the test, and at one time VOSA tried to stop discounting of fees altogether. Many stations offer a small discount coupled with a free re-test within a certain number of days, and this may be an attractive combination.

Preparing the car

Having gone to the trouble of working through the pre-test procedures in this book, it would be sensible to present the vehicle in the best possible light on the day. Clean the whole car inside and out, removing any clutter which might get in the tester's way. Reel in any loose set belts, make sure rear ones are accessible and not stuck under the seat, and that floor mats are not in a position to interfere with controls. A neat and tidy car will at least give the impression that it is cared for properly.

Getting there

It's perfectly legal to drive the car to and from a pre-arranged test without a current MoT certificate or road tax, but the vehicle must be insured. Make absolutely sure that all the details, including your name, have been recorded properly when you make the appointment, because if you're stopped en-route the Police will check with the testing station. The car must be roadworthy at all times when on the highway, and any defects will still result in a fine or points on your licence regardless of your destination. If you

are caught driving without a valid MoT certificate at any other time, the current fine is £60 if issued by the Police, rising to up to a possible £1000 if referred to court.

Paperwork

There's no requirement to have any paperwork with you, although it may be sensible to have the old certificate even if it has expired, plus the logbook just in case a problem should arise. It's possible to have any days remaining on the current certificate added to a new one, all of which will be done on the computer.

Should I stay or go?

If you have a firm appointment time then waiting for the car should not be a problem as the test should only take around 45 minutes, and many stations have a waiting room for customers. If you wish to watch the procedure there will be a viewing area available, a function which may be shared with the waiting room. Whether this option is worthwhile is open to debate as some testers don't like being watched, especially as VOSA inspectors do pose as normal customers to check up on standards. Staying could equally result in a fairer test so the decision is yours. If you do decide to watch, you aren't allowed to distract or interrupt the tester in any way.

six
The aftermath

The pass certificate (VT20)

In a bid to make the process more environmentally friendly and cheaper, MoT paperwork now comes on plain, white printer paper. The details are held online in a central database, and is accessible by various government agencies, so the need for a complicated paper version has diminished. These new forms arrived on the 16th October 2011, but the older green versions remain valid until a new test is undertaken.

The main information printed on them remains pretty much the same as before – the name of the station and the tester who carried out the work, vehicle make and model, along with VIN number, recorded mileage, and, of course, the issue and expiry dates. MoT status can be checked online at www.direct.gov.uk/yourmotcheck, and VOSA clearly states on its website that confirmation online is the ONLY guarantee of the car's status, and that

the paper printout should not be relied upon.

If you're the forgetful type, you can text the MoT certificate number to 66848, the VOSA reminder line, which, for the princely sum of £1.50, will then send prompts to your mobile phone as the test date looms. This service needs to be renewed each year.

Advisory notes

These are now printed on the pass certificate, rather than being supplied on a separate sheet, which could be advantageous to car buyers as any looming problems may be clearly listed. A sensible owner will regard advisories as a helpful prompt to rectify the defects as soon as is practical.

The refusal to issue a test certificate (VT30)

This sheet, which is more commonly referred to as the 'fail certificate,' is now printed on plain paper, just like the

MOT Test Certificate   VOSA ⚠

Vehicle & Operator Services Agency

Advisory Information

MOT Test Number

Odometer Reading

Make

Vehicle Registration Mark

Model

Colour

Vehicle Identification Number

Issuer's name

Test Class

Signature of Issuer

Expiry Date

Issued

Additional Information

Inspection Authority

Test Station

An executive agency of the Department for
Transport

About this document
1 This document is a receipt style certificate telling you that an MOT Test pass result has been recorded on The Vehicle & Operator Services Agency's (VOSA's) database of MOT Test results; this may be verified at www.direct.gov.uk/yourmotcheck
2 A test certificate relates only to the condition of the components examined at the time of test. It does not confirm the vehicle will remain roadworthy for the validity of the certificate
3 Check carefully that the details are correct.
4 Whilst advisory items listed above do not constitute MOT failure items they are drawn to your attention for advice only.
5 For further information about this document please visit www.direct.gov.uk/mot or contact VOSA on 0300 123 9000*
*Your call may be monitored or recorded for lawful purposes.

Page - end of MOT documents   VT20/templatename

The latest test certificates are simply printed on plain paper. To check their validity, you must go online.

pass certificate. It will list items which failed to reach the standard expected, although the wording of these reasons may be a little obscure to the average owner, so read them carefully whilst at the MoT station rather than leaving immediately under a cloud. Most testers will usually be perfectly happy to give a clearer explanation of why they failed a particular component.

Re-test
If your car fails the test on the windscreen and/or washers, horn, indicators/hazard lights, reflectors, lights, headlight aim, VIN number, exhaust emissions, seats, seatbelts, doors/boot lids, mirrors, ABS warning light, brake pedal rubbers, steering wheel, wheels and tyres, fuel filler cap, and last but not least numberplates, then as long as they are repaired and

the car re-submitted before the end of the next working day, those items alone can be re-checked free of charge.

If you decide to leave the car with the testing station to be repaired, a partial re-test is carried out and there will not be a re-test fee either.

If the car is removed and it fails on any other item not on the list above, a re-test fee of up to half the amount set by VOSA for a full test may apply, as long as the car is returned within ten working days.

If it's not re-submitted within that time, a full test will be required once more. Obviously this opens up the possibility of the car failing again if something else has subsequently stopped working, so make sure to at least check the obvious stuff again, such as lights, before sending it back in.

It is perfectly possible that if you

Refusal of an MOT Test Certificate

VOSA
Vehicle & Operator Services Agency

Advisory Information

MOT Test Number

Odometer Reading

Approx First Use

Registration Mark

Make

Model

Test Class

Colour

Vehicle Identification Number

I certify that for the reason(s) shown below the vehicle was not shown to comply with the statutory requirements.

Inspection Authority

Issued

Test Station

About this document
1 This document tells you that your vehicle has not been shown to meet the minimum legal requirements for the reason(s) detailed. If you intend to use your vehicle on the road you should have it repaired without delay and have it retested before the existing test validity expires.
2 Please keep this failure notice and produce it at the Testing Station in the event of a re-examination.
3 Whilst advisory items listed above do not constitute MOT failure items they are drawn to your attention for advice only.
4 Further information on retest fees or if you disagree with the test result can be found on the Fees and Appeals poster displayed in every vehicle testing station, by visiting www.direct.gov.uk/mot or contacting VOSA on 0300 123 9000*.
*Your call may be monitored or recorded for lawful purposes.

Signature of Issuer

Issuer's Name

An executive agency of the Department for **Transport**

Page - end of MOT documents

Failure certificates will list all the defects found during the inspection, and also the re-test details.

submitted your car early for the test then the old MoT certificate is still in force. It remains valid until its expiry date despite any recent fail, but if the car is unroadworthy it will remain an offence to use it on the roads, regardless of MoT status.

Complaints
If you feel that the reasons for failure are wrong, or that the test was carried out incorrectly, speak to the staff at the station first to ensure that all the relevant information has been supplied to you. If that does not resolve the situation to your satisfaction, then form VT 17 Notice of Appeal (which must be stocked by all testing stations) can be filled in and submitted to VOSA before 14 working days have elapsed. You can also initiate the process by contacting VOSA by phone on 0300 123 9000.

VOSA will wish to inspect the car and will contact you with a time and place for that to happen within five working days of receipt of your intention to appeal. For obvious reasons, you must not repair or alter the car in any way before this appeals test has taken place. This new inspection will be charged at the full rate, but this may be refundable in full or in part depending on the outcome of the inspection.

Lost it
If you should misplace your certificate, the station which tested the car can issue a duplicate, though it can charge up to £10 for this service. The station will need the registration number of the vehicle and the certificate number (or take along the V5 registration document).

Life goes on
Once a pass certificate has been obtained, there's a great temptation to forget all about the MoT for another year. However, it would be wise to incorporate at least the easier checks contained in this book into part of your regular servicing regime; the items are all safety-related after all, so keep checking!

Appendix 1

The following list explains some of the acronyms and other terms you may come across in the MoT handbook or on a failure certificate. It makes no claims to be exhaustive.

ABS
Anti-lock braking systems rely on a central computerised control unit which reads information from the wheel hubs, usually via cables. If one wheel slows more rapidly than the others during braking, an indication that it is about to lock-up, the control unit releases braking pressure to that wheel until a balance between all four is reached. This braking assessment is carried out many times a second, and the only sensation that the driver may experience is a slight vibration through the brake pedal. The reaction times of the setup are faster than a human can achieve, and so, in an emergency situation, the amount of braking force safely applied to the road surface is increased, resulting in shorter stopping distances.

Carbon monoxide
A product of incomplete combustion, usually caused by an overly rich fuel-to-air mixture. It's an odourless gas and is extremely dangerous to humans. In a correctly-functioning engine, the oxygen sensor, combined with the catalytic converter, should prevent excessive emissions of this gas.

Dual fuel
Applies to vehicles capable of running on two fuel sources; usually, but not exclusively, petrol and LPG. Most cars with this capacity feature aftermarket conversion kits, although some manufacturers offered this option from new.

EPB
Electric parking brakes can be fully-electronic (relying on a signal to the rear

brakes to operate an electric motor), or partly mechanical (where a motor is used to pull the handbrake cables).

EPS (or EPAS)
A computer-controlled steering assistance system which relies on an electric motor rather than a power steering pump and fluid.

HID headlights
The HID stands for high intensity discharge and, unlike normal headlights, these use an electric arc to generate a more intense light. They run at high voltage, so care should be taken when working on the system. If you're unsure that your vehicle has them fitted there are a few telltale signs. On the rear of the unit there will be a ignitor module, and the reflector may be marked DCR. They also take a couple of seconds to reach full intensity and, once properly lit, have a slightly blue tint to the light.

Hydrocarbons
These are emitted from your engine due to incomplete burning of the fuel. Misfires, engine wear, and/or an overly lean mixture can all increase the hydrocarbon emissions. They are responsible for causing respiratory problems in congested areas, and are a main contributor to smog.

Lambda
The optimum air-to-fuel ratio in a petrol-engined car is approximately 14.7-to-1, respectively. In order to maintain that ratio, a lambda sensor reads the mixture when the engine is running and signals the car's electronic control unit to constantly alter fuel delivery to keep everything at the right level. Lambda probes soot up, and sometimes cleaning the operating surface may eliminate a problem if it is slight. Replacement is the only other option.

LPG
Liquid petroleum gas is an alternative fuel currently available at an advantageous price thanks to having less tax imposed on it compared to other road fuels; a result of its cleaner burning and, therefore, environmental benefits. This financial advantage may not continue.

Traction control
A system which monitors the amount of slip permitted at the wheel before corrective action is taken to regain grip. It's often part of a computer-controlled ABS system.

TPMS
Tyre pressure monitoring systems illuminate a warning light on the dashboard when the car's tyre pressures are low. On vehicles used after January 2012, the circuit will be checked for operation, and will fail if the light fails to go out with the engine running. For private owners, the test will obviously only become an issue after three years (January 2015).

VOSA
Part of the Department of Transport, VOSA is responsible for running the MoT system. There is a lot of useful information on the website, with various downloads available, including the full *MoT Inspection Manual*.

Appendix 2

VOSA includes two diagrams in the *Inspection Manual* indicating the areas where corrosion is to be regarded as structural, and these are reproduced here. As stated in the main text, however, for the ordinary car owner, all holes should be repaired, rather than risk a debate over what should or shouldn't be included on the day.

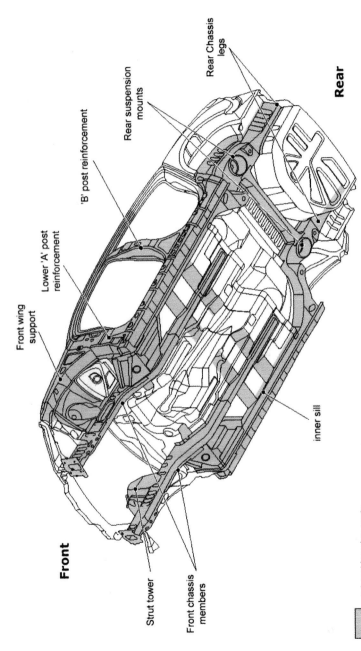

Front

Rear

Rear Chassis legs

Rear suspension mounts

'B' post reinforcement

Lower 'A' post reinforcement

Front wing support

Strut tower

Front chassis members

inner sill

= Load bearing parts

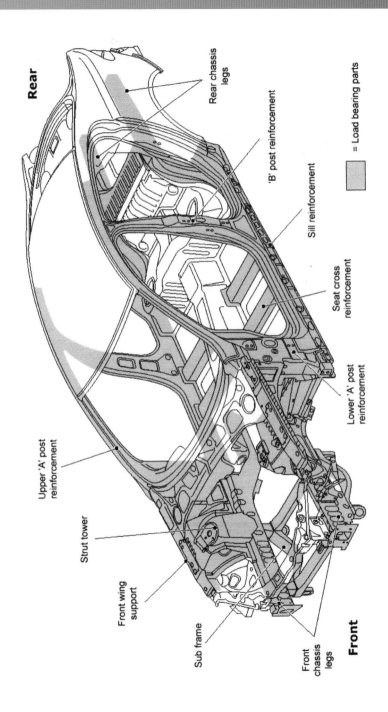

Rear

Rear chassis legs

'B' post reinforcement

Sill reinforcement

= Load bearing parts

Seat cross reinforcement

Lower 'A' post reinforcement

Upper 'A' post reinforcement

Strut tower

Front wing support

Sub frame

Front chassis legs

Front

ISBN: 978-1-845843-51-9
Paperback • 21x14.8cm • £9.99* UK/$19.95* USA • 96 pages • 32 colour pictures

For more info on Veloce titles, visit our website at www.veloce.co.uk •
email: info@veloce.co.uk • Tel: +44(0)1305 260068
* prices subject to change, p&p extra

ISBN: 978-1-845843-88-5
Paperback • 21x14.8cm • £9.99* UK/$19.95* USA • 80 pages • 115 colour
pictures

For more info on Veloce titles, visit our website at www.veloce.co.uk •
email: info@veloce.co.uk • Tel: +44(0)1305 260068
* prices subject to change, p&p extra

ISBN: 978-1-845843-96-0
Paperback • 21x14.8cm • £9.99* UK/$19.95* USA • 96 pages • 177 colour
pictures

For more info on Veloce titles, visit our website at www.veloce.co.uk •
email: info@veloce.co.uk • Tel: +44(0)1305 260068
* prices subject to change, p&p extra

Index